Victorian Lowestoft

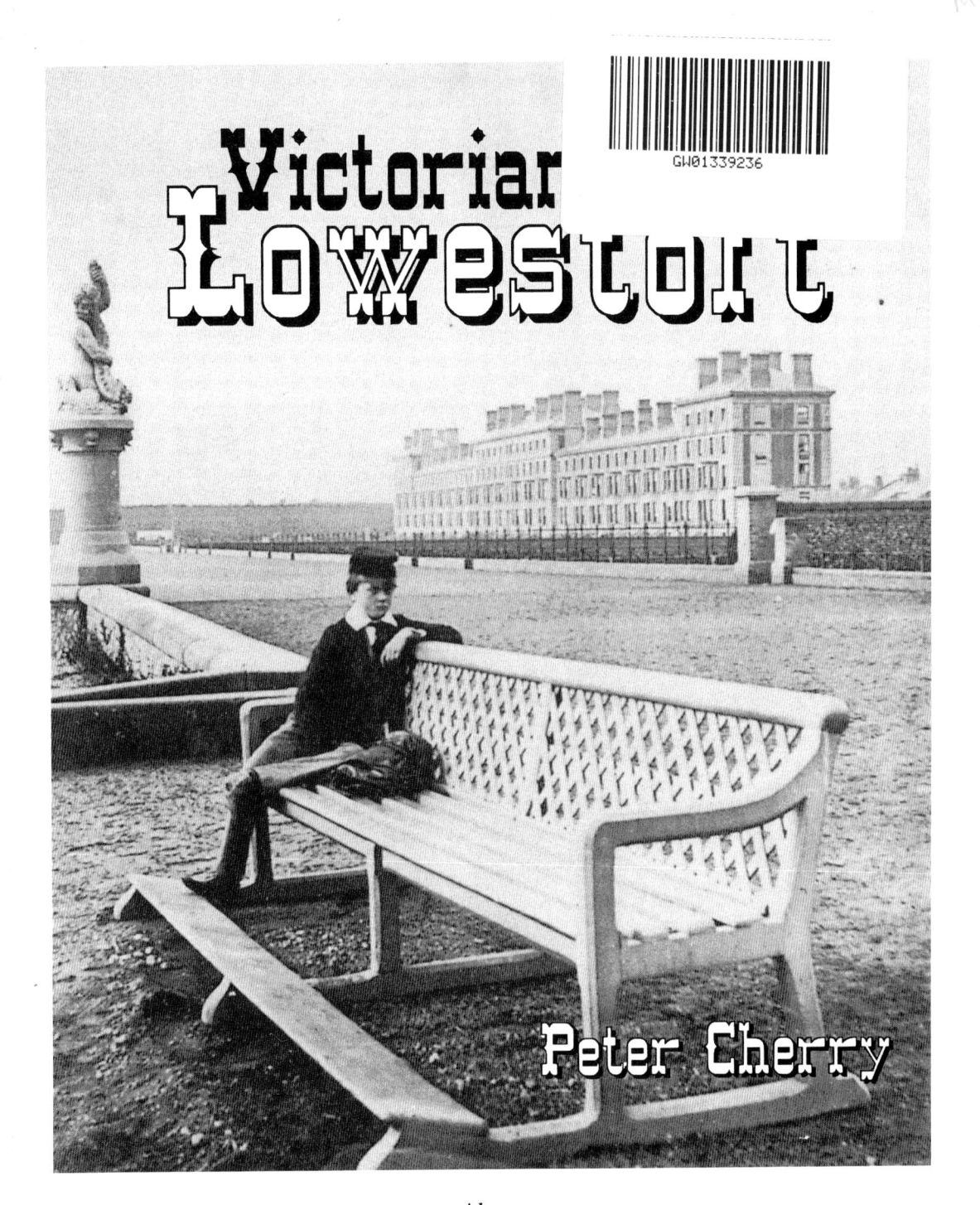

Peter Cherry

Above:
A view of about 1860 of one of Peto's elegant terraces which graced the new Esplanade which he also built.

Front Cover:
Sail still dominated trade at the port in the late 19th century, but steam tugs made entering harbour less hazardous in times of storms and calms. Here the barquentine *'Alice Sterry'* is towed through-bridge by the tug *'Despatch'*.

Published by:
PETER CHERRY,
40 White's Lane,
Kessingland,
Lowestoft,
Suffolk NR33 3TG

© *Peter Cherry 1992*

ISBN 0 9502474 1 3

No part of this book may be reprinted or reproduced in any form or by any means, either electronic, mechanical, photocopying or recording, or in any information storage and retrieval system, without prior permission in writing from the publisher.

Printed by:
COLOUR PRINT,
The Drift,
Fakenham,
Norfolk

Acknowledgement

My thanks to the staff of the Suffolk Record Office at Lowestoft and Ipswich for their help in my research for this book — and for permission to reproduce the photographs of Oulton Broad Ice Carnival and the wreck of the *Elbe*.

Introduction

At the beginning of the 19th century Lowestoft was a 'small, obscure fishing village of some 2,000 souls' wrote Mr. A. E. Murton in the Lowestoft Journal in 1901. The history of that period was 'wrapped in obscurity' he added. But it was known that there was a total of 450 homes, many of them in High Street, the rest — some mere huts — huddled together on the north beach.

Open land ran down from High Street to the marshes of Lake Lothing and south of that was only scrubland and marram hills. All this was to change dramatically when Norwich quarrelled with Yarmouth and decided to create a new route to the sea by building a harbour at Lowestoft. This was opened in 1831, but almost immediately Norwich patched up its quarrel with the Norfolk port — and left Lowestoft to rot. It was well on the way to extinction in 1843 when Samuel Morton Peto, the great Victorian railway contractor, took over. He not only brought the railway to the town and improved the harbour, but also set about the task of creating a new holiday resort. Early 19th century Lowestoft may be 'wrapped in obscurity' but we know much more about that exciting Peto era, the more so because it coincided with the development of photography. Michael Barrett was the town's first photographer and we owe to him many of the pictures of Victorian Lowestoft in this collection.

Peto's vigour and enterprise transformed Lowestoft from 'an obscure fishing village' into a thriving town. When, in 1897, the country celebrated Queen Victoria's Diamond Jubilee, Lowestoft did so with a fervour which also reflected its pride in its own 'Sixty Glorious Years' in which it had become a Borough with a population of 30,000, the fourth biggest fishing port in the country and an important holiday resort.

The census of 1901 records a population of 29,850. Out of a working population of just over 12,000, well over 2,000 men were employed in fishing and ancillary trades, while nearly 1,500 women were in domestic service. An indication that the town was still expanding is evident from the 1,216 building workers. Fashion was obviously important in a seaside resort for there were 472 milliners and dressmakers.

This is by no means an attempt to write a history of the town, merely to try to give something of the flavour of that Victorian era — the harbour, the fishing industry, the elegant seaside terraces and, in some of the pictures, a fleeting glance at the creations of all those dressmakers and milliners.

Many of Peto's Victorian buildings remain, but too often I have had to record, with sadness, 'pulled down ...'. One hopes that we may now be able to save what is left.

Peter Cherry

Fishing from the beach

Although Lowestoft in the early 19th century has been described as 'an obscure fishing village', it was, in fact, a thriving coastal fishing centre as this drawing by E. Duncan shows. Fishing boats and merchant ships landed their fish and cargoes on the beach and there was a ship building industry on the Denes.

At home in a boat

Even after the building of the harbour many of the smaller fishing boats and yawls continued to work from the beach. This print of 1854 shows a picturesque huddle of 'shods'. Reminiscent of Dickens' 'Peggotty' some of the fisherfolk made their homes in half boats. From one such a watch is being kept on the sea. The Beachmen were ever alert to the chance of vessels in trouble — and salvage.

The Port

A tranquil scene in the life of the port in the 1860s. These were the cattle sheds built for the new trade in livestock with Denmark. At first the trade in cattle and sheep from across the North Sea proved prosperous but eventually the North Europe Steam Navigation Company collapsed. A memorable disaster was when the iron paddle boat *Tonning* blew up as she approached the harbour. It is remembered not so much for the fact that eleven Lowestoft men were killed, but for the bonanza of free joints of beef and mutton!

Battery Green

Battery Green seen from Old Nelson Street in 1874. It was Henry VIII who ordered bulwarks and guns to be set up here to defend, not Lowestoft, but the channel to the important Yarmouth anchorage. For over three centuries Lowestoft panicked at every emergency — from the Spanish Armada to the Crimean War. Earthworks were repaired and the guns dug up. They never went into action, the only excitement being that several of the rusty guns blew up during practice firing. Finally, around 1880, the battery became a park, now the site of a multi-storey car park.

The Old Reading Room

A barque which looks as though it may have been a storm casualty and is up for sale, lying in the outer harbour about 1870. The Reading Room on the South Pier, and part of the pier itself, was destroyed by fire in June 1885. The Reading Room was the centre of entertainment for visiting gentry. 'Balls are held during the Season which cannot fail to prove a great attraction of the votaries of terpsichore' declared one writer.

Conrad was here

The inner harbour, a forest of masts in 1874, much as novelist Joseph Conrad would have known it when he first set foot on English soil here in 1878. 'Polish Joe', who was to become a master of English literature, was taught the language by Captain Isiah Munnings, Master of the collier *Skimmer of the Seas*. Was it gratitude which prompted Conrad to declare later in life that the finest English was to be heard in the streets of Lowestoft?

The Harbour Bridge

Lowestoft's original harbour bridge seen from the south about 1870. Taken before the building of the Bridge Terrace of houses and shops, the picture gives an unimpeded view across to Commercial Road where among the premises was that of Rayson, Chemist and Druggist. Even at this time the bridge was proving far too narrow for the increasing traffic, but it was not until 1897 that it was replaced by a new bridge.

The 'New' Bridge

Lowestoft's new bridge goes into position in 1897. In its day it was the fastest operating swing bridge in the country. Crowds gathered for the opening ceremony with leading citizens jostling for the honour of being first across. In the event they were all beaten by a lad on a bike. This bridge did duty for over 70 years, but grew steadily more troublesome. Chaos reigned when it finally jammed in January 1969. The town was cut in two and it was six weeks before a temporary bridge was thrown across the harbour. The present double bascule bridge, itself not without its faults, was opened in March 1972.

Sea-water For Sale

In 1880 the GER, which had seen Lowestoft become one of the country's premier fishing ports, hit upon a new idea — selling sea-water. Customers could have a three-gallon keg delivered for sixpence — and the railway often despatched 2,000 a day. It was intended for baths, but, despite the fact that it all came from the harbour, some people drank it! There was a piped supply to the station, but sometimes a bucket on a rope was used to fill the kegs. This odd trade was killed by W.W.II. A pity since we still had plenty left!

The Outer Harbour

Originally the port consisted of a small outer harbour between two short piers, but when he took over Peto lengthened these to create a larger refuge. This was the outer harbour in the 1860s. On the left can be seen the old Reading Room and the Royal Hotel. A dredger, possibly the *Excavator,* is at work in what is now the yacht basin.

A Rival To Sail

Steam was already threatening sail at the turn of the century, but there were still plenty of sailing smacks in service as shown in this shot of the trawl dock and yacht basin. Indeed, the last sailing smacks did not disappear from the port until after the last war.

The New Waveney Dock

With the growth of the fishing industry an addition to the harbour became imperative. Opened in 1883, the new Waveney Dock and fish market soon became the heart of the industry. Houses were going up on the old Grove Estate in the late 1880s, but those fronting Whapload Road were yet to come when this picture was taken.

The Old Ice House

The rise of the fishing industry meant a huge increase in the demand for ice, much of it shipped from Norway. Here, in the 1880s, a barque unloads its huge blocks of ice at the thatched ice house near the bridge. Insulated by thick layers of sawdust it would last well into the summer. The manufacture at the port of cheaper 'artificial ice' meant the end of this trade and the old ice house was demolished in 1911.

The Ice Carnival

The last decades of the 19th century saw a series of hard winters. In 1891 a sheep was roasted on the frozen Oulton Broad and there were sleigh rides during a great Ice Carnival. The money raised went to the hospital. There was hardship too. In 1881 soup kitchens had served 600 meals a day to the cold and hungry. There was another Ice Carnival in February 1895 when a bullock and sheep were roasted on the Broad.

Black Saturday

Black Saturday, October 1882 — anchored in the lee of the South Pier are two survivors from a ferocious gale and huge seas which battered the east coast and in which countless lives were lost. Thirteen vessels were lost between Lowestoft and Covehithe alone. At the height of the gale the Lowestoft lifeboat men refused to launch because of a grievance about non-payment of previous claims. It was only after the townspeople had threatened to smash in the lifeboat shed doors and put to sea themselves that, under the great Coxswain Bob Hook, the lifeboat men launched and saved seven lives.

The Old Company

Figureheads and name boards are displayed, rather like hard-won trophies, on the 'shod' on the north beach of the Old Company of Beachmen in the 1890s. These hardy seafarers, with their fast yawls, relied chiefly on the salvage of wrecks for a living, each man who took part receiving a share. Hard men they were, but many of the Beachmen had a rule that at least one share was to go to the poor and needy.

The Lifeboat Crew

The crew of the lifeboat *Samuel Plimsoll* in 1890, all wearing their Captain Ward's patent cork lifebelts. In practice some of the lifeboat men, although they could not swim, did not like wearing the lifebelts finding them cumbersome and restrictive. Many fishermen refused to learn to swim saying that if they went overboard they preferred a quick death to the prolonged agony of fighting for life. The *Samuel Plimsoll* was replaced in 1905 by the *Kentwell*, the last sailing lifeboat on the station.

Wreck of the Elbe

When the crack German transatlantic liner *Elbe* sank in the North Sea off Lowestoft in January 1895 only 20 people survived, including a lone woman. The liner had gone down quickly after a collision 40 miles off the port with the merchant ship *Craigie*. Over 300 people died that night and the handful of survivors owed their lives to Skipper George Wright and the crew of the smack *Wildflower* which snatched them from the icy seas. They received presentation gold watches from the German Emperor. Fine Dresden china from packing cases swept ashore is still treasured in some Lowestoft families.

Corncross Chapel

The centre of local trade, administration and worship for over three centuries, the Corncross Chapel stood on the site of the present Town Hall. Built in 1570 and replaced by this building in 1698 it was finally pulled down in 1874 to make way for a new Town Hall. Interestingly, because of its original use as a chapel, the parish church of St. Margaret's has a permanent right to hold meetings in the Town Hall which replaced it, a right last exercised by the Rev. Bill Westwood in April, 1965.

Town Hall

This was the new Town Hall in the 1880s, flanked by pubs on each corner of the building. Handy one might think for a refreshing draught after a long evening meeting. But, in fact, the Improvement Commissioners — forerunners of the Borough Council — used to meet at eight o'clock in the morning. They found it concentrated the minds of the members wonderfully if they had a business to attend to — and kept discussions short and to the point!

High Street 'Haunt of Vice'

The upper end of High Street in the 1890s appears to be a highly respectable mixture of houses and shops, but in 1887 the Mayor was urged to take action when one councillor declared: 'There are houses in High Street and around it which equal the worst haunts of vice in any part of the Continent'. By the time this postcard appeared work had already started on pulling down property on the west side — not to sweep away 'haunts of vice', but to widen the road.

Town Crier

In the days before radio, TV or popular national newspapers, the Town Crier was important to a town. Nathan Garner filled the office at Lowestoft in 1880, a man known for his stentorian voice and his ability to stand stock still, like a waxworks figure, for minutes on end. He was also known for his refusal to 'cry down women'. This service, paid for by the husband, entailed warnings cried through the town that Mrs. So-and-So was not to be served drink or allowed 'tick'. Nathan would have nothing to do with such commissions!

Postman

The horses and carts stopped and everyone came to their doors, even Postman John Rand paused on his round of deliveries for this picture of High Street in 1898. Cottages on the left were already coming down to make way for the widening of the road.

Pawnbroker Shot

Samuel Angood, who ran the pawnbroker's shop next door to the Seaview Hotel in High Street, nearly signed his death warrant when he accepted a pistol as a pledge in 1865. Unredeemed, the pistol was entered in an auction in Norwich. The Lot was called, the porter picked up the pistol and accidentally pulled the trigger and shot Mr. Angood through the head. He fell seriously wounded, but survived.

The Three Herrings

Arnold House, on the right, still stands, but all other property in the scene of 1892 has gone, including the pub The Three Herrings on the immediate left, which stood on the site of an earlier pub, the Hole in the Wall.

Grisly Discovery

Not a post-war pre-fab, but the temporary home of the Three Herrings which was pulled down in the course of road widening in 1898. When the pub was demolished the skeletons of some sixty horses were found beneath the ground floor. No explanation has ever been found for this extraordinary discovery.

High Street

Some of the shop fronts may have changed and the elegant cast iron pissoir on the left has disappeared, but this section of High Street looks much the same today as it did when this photograph was taken in the 1890s. Even the clock over Crake's shop is still there, though not working.

Gravestones Shock

When the huddle of old cottages on the Triangle were demolished towards the end of the last century it was discovered that gravestones from St, Margaret's churchyard had been used as hearthstones. Demanding that a close watch be kept in future, the Lowestoft Journal commented: 'It is not nice for Lowestoftians to imagine that in the future the tangible remembrances of departed loved relatives might be used for the base of a fireplace'.

Grove Estate

Looking across the fish market in the late 1880s when the sale of the Grove Estate and its six acres opened the way for development on the east side of London Road North. At the top of the picture can be seen earlier building. Left to right: Suffolk Hotel, Suffolk Terrace, Lloyd's Bank, Post Office and National Provincial Bank. The wooden buildings in the foreground are: Yarmouth Stores, Cooper Bros., Seamen's Mission and Reading Room.

Shopping Centre

London Road North, looking south in the 1870s. Large residences had already gone up on the west side, but development to the east was delayed until the sale of the Grove Estate, the wall and trees of which can be seen on the left. Many of the old houses on the right of this shopping street are still there, their upper storeys peeping above the new shop fronts.

17

Fisher's Lodging House

Another view of what is now the main shopping centre in the 1870s, this time looking north. It was taken from a spot almost opposite the Tesco Store. On the right can be seen the upper floors of Marine Terrace, now shops and offices. It was here, at Fisher's Lodging House, that poet Edward Fitzgerald stayed during his frequent visits to the town — and to his fisherman friend 'Posh' Fletcher. Fitzgerald once described it as 'ugly old Lowestoft'. He should see it now!

The Railway Station

Peto's liking for the Italianate style can be judged from this picture of the 1870s which includes the north facade of the old railway station. The coming of the railway had prompted development in the 1850s and 60s, including the building of the Imperial Hotel.

Denmark Road

Denmark Road — a name which commemorates the cattle trade with Denmark — in the 1870s. These were the days before metalled roads and conditions were bad, particularly for those on foot. Hence the provision of cobbled crossings amid what, in winter, was a sea of mud.

The Suffolk Hotel

The popular coaching inn, the Suffolk Hotel, is up for sale in the 1870s. 'These eligible plots of land to be let on building leases' says the notice. The coming of the railway had hit the coaching inns hard. When, in 1847, London and Norwich were linked by rail 700 horses, which plied the Turnpike, were redundant, along with thousands of coach drivers, ostlers and servants at the coaching inns.

Peto's New Town

Peto, who took over the ailing harbour in 1844, saw great possibilities at Lowestoft. He had his eye on the vast expanse of scrubland to the south of the bridge and, having wined and dined leading citizens at Somerleyton Hall, he offered £200 for the lot. They jumped at it. Then he unrolled his plans for the development of what amounted to a 'new town'. Much of what he built remains including Marine Terrace, pictured in 1874, which was described as 'second class dwellings'.

Wellington Esplanade

More imposing were the 'first class' residences of Wellington Esplanade fronted by their own communal park of Wellington Gardens. Pictured in 1874, the gardens have yet to be laid out. Restrictive covenants mean that the Gardens can never be built on — a very wise move on the part of Peto.

St. John's Church

London Road South in 1875. Like many of the oldest pictures in this book, this was the work of Michael Barrett. Photography in those days involved lengthy exposures and Barrett seems to have had a team of lads trained to stand motionless for the necessary time. Peto built, and paid for, St. John's Church to serve his new town, It was completed in 1854 and was demolished in 1978.

Kirkley Water Tower

It was in 1852 that a meeting was held to consider bringing a supply of sweet water to Lowestoft and work started in 1853. But little Kirkley had stolen a march on its big brother. It had had a supply of water — and gas — since the 1840s. This was Kirkley water tower. In the background is Kirkley St. Peter's which was transformed by major restoration and building later in the century.

Christ Church

The Victorian era was one of great church building by all denominations and elaborate restorations of existing churches. Among the many new churches was Christ Church built to serve the rapidly growing Beach Village and opened in February 1869. It was claimed that a quarter of the town's population at the time lived 'On the Grit' and the community deserved a church of its own. Today the Beach Village has disappeared under new industry and has few residents, but Christ Church still has a loyal following.

The Baptist Church

Another new church was that of the Baptists whose old church was sited near the present Journal office. It was one of the first buildings to go up on the Grove Estate and was opened in 1899. The site is now occupied by Boots and the Baptists have a new church on the corner of Kirkley Park Road.

The Cholera Epidemic

Improvement in public health was a major concern in Victorian Lowestoft which was swept by savage epidemics of cholera, typhoid and smallpox. The first hospital was opened in 1840 on what is now St. Margaret's Plain. The present hospital replaced it in 1882. But epidemics continued to rage in a town in which so many people drew their water from shallow wells. Mr. R. B. Nicholson, who was to become our first town clerk, recalled that when he arrived in 1873 the town had passed through a smallpox epidemic so severe that uncoffined bodies had been taken by cart to the churchyard.

The Convalescent Home

Lowestoft Convalescent Home at the turn of the century. Originally a boys' school it was taken over by the Home in 1877 and subsequently enlarged. A large part of the grounds is now occupied by the Trinity Methodist Church.

The Yacht Club

In 1859 'a few boating gentlemen', concerned about unruly behaviour at Water Frolics and other sailing events, met to form the Norfolk and Suffolk Yacht Club in the hope of exercising some control of future racing. The new club, which was later to gain the prefix 'Royal' established its headquarters at Lowestoft where, in 1885, it built this clubhouse. This served until 1903 when, with the building of the present headquarters, the old one was moved lock, stock and barrel to Crown Meadow where it served the Town Football Club for over 80 years.

Sailing Safety

The first safety boat of the Norfolk and Suffolk Yacht Club ready for launching in the 1860s. The clubhouse had not then been built and there was a fine shelving beach into what is now the yacht basin. In the background are the Royal Stables.

North End Common

North End Common c1870. The first mansions on what is now North Parade had gone up — and were proving difficult to sell. The common was said to be 'the resort of unruly elements' but within a few years it had been transformed into the elegant arboretum of Belle Vue Park. The pile of stones on the right is said to have been the base of the old beacon fires which gave warning to shipping before the building of the first lighthouse.

Belle Vue Park

It was a day for best bonnets and gowns for the ladies and top hats for the gentlemen when Belle Vue Park was officially opened in May 1874. One policeman, it seems, was sufficient to control the crowds and he is prudent enough to have stationed himself near to a group of youngsters who might well include 'unruly elements'!

The Old Highlight

A striking feature which adds greatly to the charm of Belle Vue and Sparrow's Nest parks is the Highlight, shown here in the 1860s. Built in 1676 by the order of diarist Samuel Pepys, then Master of Trinity House, it was modernised several times before being replaced by the present lighthouse in 1874. It was a coveted posting for keepers since it was a 'man and wife station' where, after lonely years on isolated lights, they were able to have their family with them.

Sparrow's Nest

When the town council bought Sparrow's Nest for £12,000 in 1897 it became one of the town's most popular pleasure grounds. At first a large marquee sufficed for concert parties, but frequently it blew down. In 1913 a new Grand Pavilion was built, pulled down in 1992. In 1939 the Park and Pavilion were taken over as HMS Europa and became the base of the R.N. Minesweepers. In the fight against the mines and U-Boats HMS Europa lost almost 500 ships — losses far in excess of any other branch of the Royal Navy.

A Romantic Old House

Sparrow's Nest has a long and romantic history. It was the home in the early 1800s of Robert Sparrow, one of the founders of the Suffolk Humane Society, forerunner of the modern lifeboat service. Later it was the home of Baron Alderson. It was here that Lord Robert Cecil met and wooed his future wife, Miss Alderson. The old house was pulled down in 1963, but few people missed it as over the years it had been hidden by other buildings.

The Ravine

The Ravine in the 1870s was little more than a rough track down a break-neck hill. At the bottom can be seen the boundary wall of Sparrow's Nest, then known as Cliff Cottage. Rising on the near right is the old site of the North Battery, built by order of Henry VIII.

Children's Corner

Holidaymakers at the turn of the century had no need of the medical advice to stay clear of too much sunbathing. With their umbrellas, long dresses and bonnets they looked well protected from the harmful rays. Even the children kept their hats and coats on. Indeed, it was not until the 1920s that sun lovers began casting precautions — and clothing — to the winds.

Bathing Machines

From the middle of the 18th century until early this century bathing machines were an inseparable part of the seaside scene, having been introduced to Lowestoft in 1769. They were described as screening the bathers from 'the most inquisitive eye'. Victorian Lowestoft had an imposing row on the south beach, but they were scrapped in 1913 as being 'out of keeping with a modern resort'.

The Royal Hotel

The Royal Hotel in the 1890s. Built in 1849 this was one of the East Coast's premier hotels. Nall, in his 1866 guide to Lowestoft and Yarmouth, described it as 'a splendid establishment' and one which had 'the requisites of an Inn of the first class'. It was pulled down in 1973. To the south a long line of villas stretches along the Esplanade. Between the wars the council pursued a policy of buying and demolishing these villas to provide a more spacious sea front. That achieved, the present council seems set on developing it again.

Warren House and Denes

The Denes about 1870. Warren House at the bottom of what is now Links Road was closely associated with the Lowestoft China Factory. Here, using water power from a spring, clay was 'puddled' for the factory near the Town Hall. The spring has recently been the centre of controversy over plans to bottle and sell the water, which is said to be of a very high quality.

Home of the 'Mustard King'

Jeremiah Colman, the Norwich 'Mustard King', was among the wealthy who had summer residences on the coast. This was The Clyffe at Corton where he entertained Prime Minister Gladstone in 1890. Not a man given to levity, Gladstone never-the-less essayed a small joke when he came down to family prayers on his first morning. "Are we all 'mustered'?" he asked! Threatened by sea erosion and badly damaged by fire, The Clyffe was pulled down in 1911.

The Winter Gardens

Buying Somerleyton Hall in 1844, Sir Morton Peto transformed it into a princely residence. The Winter Garden, on the left, was one of the wonders of the age. Nall said of it 'Coleridge may have seen it when, in his charmed opium slumber, he dreamed of the palace of Kubla Khan'. Though it now lacks the Winter Gardens, which was pulled down in 1912, Somerleyton Hall remains a major tourist attraction in the area.

Almshouses

The Victorian era saw the founding of a number of almshouses in the town, but some 20 years ago those that survived gave way to modern bungalows on Church Green. Demolished around that time were Dove Court, pictured here, Thurston Road Almshouses and the Fishermen's Hospital in Whapload Road. The latter was built for 'worn out industrious fishermen' but it was laid down that the small weekly stipend could be withdrawn for 'insobriety, misbehaviour or unbecoming conduct'.

The Lighthouse Cottages

The Old Lighthouse Cottages about 1900. These picturesque cottages were probably old when Victoria came to the throne and may well have accommodated the lighthouse keepers before new houses were added to the Highlight in mid-century. During constant complaints about the constant blocking of the harbour entrance in 1896 it was claimed that in the past blockages had been caused by the dumping of debris when the new Highlight was built in 1874. They were certainly not the cottages in this picture — they lasted till 1938.

The Empire Hotel

In 1900, three years after Queen Victoria had celebrated her Diamond Jubilee, this massive hotel was opened on the heights of Kirkley Cliff. At such a time there could be no other name for it — The Empire. Britain ruled a quarter of the earth's surface and a quarter of its people. It was an Empire on which the sun never set. But the sun did not shine on the hotel and in 1920 it became St. Luke's Hospital. It did not reopen after W.W.II. The sun had set on the old British Empire when the hotel was demolished in 1958.

The End of an Era

The end of an era, 1901. Following the death of the Old Queen crowds gathered outside Lowestoft Town Hall to hear the Prince of Wales proclaimed King Edward VII.